Passive Income:

The Ultimate Beginner's Guide to Passive Income and Earning Money While You Sleep

by Lucas Arquette

Table of Contents:

Introduction – page 3
Automatic Profit Machines – page 6
Know What Sells – page 19
Research is Money – page 23
Developing A Successful Attitude – page 25
Work Smart. Not Hard. - page 29
Your Passive Income Machines - 32
It Shouldn't Feel Like Work – page 44
Reviewing Your Profitable Passive Income Machines – page 48
Be Confident, But Keep Your Ego in Check! - page 56

Successful Product Ideas – page 63

Be Responsible with Your Budget – page 67

Get Things Done! - page 71

Beyond Your First Successful Passive Income Source – page 91

All contents are protected by applicable copyright laws.

Introduction

You're here for **one** reason. You've thought about your life, and you've realized that it's time to learn more how to make money outside of the "traditional" method of being employed.

According to a released study by The American Psychological Association, it looks like a little over two out of three Americans suffer from stress revolving around the realm of money and income.

And while freeing up more money in your life starts with a great budget, there's no doubt that an average income could use a nice little boost from a business that works for you around the clock.

Passive income is a wonderful way to make personalized advanced "AI" workers work for you on holidays, weekends, while we're busy working, while we're playing, or while we're asleep.

There's **no better investment** that you're going to make.

Time or Money.... In this book I'll teach you 20 ways to create passive income with money.

Now that you know what you want to do, it's time to understand a little more about business. While most passive income systems are designed to develop a way to make money hands free, this doesn't mean that you don't have to put in some hard work up front in order to get the ball rolling.

A major part about passive income is understanding how to set up systems that create value inside of your market. In other words, the only way to make money is by creating a product or service that translates into direct exchanges of money.

Automatic Profit Machines

The first step towards making passive income a reality takes a little bit of work. However, any time that you have will be suitable. How many hours are you planning on working to create your very own "robot" that works around the clock to make you money? Do you have 1 hour a day? Three hours over the weekend? What does your free time look like? The major truth about passive income is simple. Most business experts understand and practice the power of compounding. However, unlike popular belief, this system of compounding doesn't always mean that the faster you launch, the faster you make money.

Now, your goal as you journey through passive income is simple. If you don't set up your first stream of income in 30-90 days, there's a major chance that you'll postpone your efforts towards making passive income because you've seen no physical progress towards making your passive income machines a reality.

In other words, if you're looking to become a passive income creator, you're going to have to learn how to balance and optimize the power of compounding.

The Power of Compounding

Compounding is a unique creature. Tony Robbins is a wonderful source to talk about when it comes to this subject because of his public perspective towards passive income and the power of compounding. He believes that the number one rule to financial independence isn't how much money we make. It's all about how we invest our time, skills and assets to make the most amount of money in the shortest time possible.

Why? Because it allows us to **compound**.

Passive income is the perfect way for you to make some breathing room in your income, but also become financially independent over time. For the power of this principle to work, we need to dive into the three essentials that drive compounding for passive income. It's kind of like a formula.

This math is considered conservative by professionals, but for the sake of presenting the formula, all we have to do is assume these numbers are average. After the example, we're going to dive into some insane research by SearchEngineLand in order to hone in on the importance of setting up your passive income machines correctly so you can make some good money on autopilot in the future.

These machines don't get built overnight, but they do something much more incredible. They make the development of income more static and allows for a more powerful and in depth machine to run your passive income with.

The basic formula moves as follows:
1. You launch an income that converts a little under 1% once every week.
2. You launch an income machine that converts at 3% every month.

It's easy to believe that having four machines working hard at a one percent would give you a better overall chance to succeed, right? It creates diversity and allows you to start making money.

However, let's break this down to 3 months down the road.

-You have 12 machines converting at 1%, and you have acquired 10,000 visitors to your site.

-You have 3 machines converting at 3 % with 10,000 visitors to the sites.

The overall conversion rates indicate that with the same exact customers over a longer period of time, the 3 machines will have acquired a total customer base of 300 while the 12 machines combine for only 100 customers.

But where this example gets tricky is when we choose to reinvest our profits from our business. In the example, let's suggest that we invest $1000 inside of our passive income. The first machine is available at the end of the first week, so the investment returns to the bank account in 14 days. The next go around, you made $100...so you invest $1,100 to generate $1,210 by the end of the first month.

Month 2 is where the fun begins.

You choose to drop in another $1,000 for the month. You now have $2,210 in your hand and 5 machines. You throw it all in, and you get an extra $221. The total investment runs out to be $2,431. Two weeks later, you get the money back and you get to invest it all to create a total of $2,674.10.

On the other hand, if you had to wait for an

entire 30 days to invest your money in the other systems, you find that you didn't use your $1,000 from the month before so you drop $2,000 in and invest equally in the systems from month to month. It performs three times better. It pulls in $600 allowing you to invest a total of $2,600 by day 45. The total amount at the end of month two then comes out to $3,380.

Month four is where things get start to separate. In the 3 machines, $5,712 comes in without investing an extra thousand dollars. At the same time, you chose not to invest an extra thousand for the dozen machines you have available. You reinvest your total earnings from the system and you get a total of $3,235.54. In other words, making income as fast as possible failed in terms of utilizing the true power of compounding.

In other words, the fastest way to making money isn't always the fastest way to making good money.

You may still be tempted to overlook the importance of research inside of your passive income machines. It's easy to overlook and most professionals around the world probably did this from time to time. However, pros look at what works and they implement it. Before you dive into building income machines, we have to look at research from SearchEngineLand.

It brings the importance of optimal compounding to life. No one wants to work more than they have to while creating passive income. Life is busy enough. However, after reading more about this research, I'm positive you'll be convinced about the importance of research.

The advantages of taking the time to launch a better machine.
The advantages of rapidly seeing money.
A great way to use time management to balance the two. In other words, there's a perfect balance to launch your business based on the way to get yourself moving.

If you want to make money through passive income, it's crucial that no matter what happens, you launch a passive income machine within 30 days. 30 days from this very second. This will allow you enough time to develop a better passive income machine while you create results.

Here are a couple of realities you face when you skip out on research.

This market analysis is for online businesses; however, it translates into every market and passive income that you install. In the research, about one of four accounts were working at a conversion rate of less than 1%.

The average across rate throughout combining all of the industries was approximately 2.35%. However, there's a crowd that's killing it. The best part is that it's not as exclusive as what you think. The top quarter of the accounts were converting at a minimum of 5.31%. This means that 25% of accounts were operating two times better than the industry standard. Not 1%, 5%, or 10%. That's a huge portion of the market.

But what's the difference between the two? The answer is simple. They don't have a magic wand shipped over from J.K. Rowling or a secret software algorithm telling them what to do. Your biggest competition might have a million-dollar copywriter working for them.

Every time I dabble into the market, I discover more about how good the competition is. If I find myself overwhelmed, I just sit back and relax. One in four businesses make a killing online. All the money isn't ruled by the best businesses inside of the industry!

When it comes to compounding, setting up high quality passive income machines once a month conquers a collection of tiny low performing automated machines.

You're not going to automatically break into the top 10% right out of the gate simply through research. However, it looks like landing pages in the top 10% actually convert above 10%. At this point, it should be clear that you're looking to create a workforce. Instead of having a bunch of low performing machines, investing time to approach the market is crucial towards creating a quality income with every project you pick up.

When you go through and start researching your competitors and you look for ways to acquire money, you'll find some pretty helpful tools available for free. However, most changes that have to do with small tweaks you can do to transform your business.

While these tips are helpful, it's important to understand that major changes in conversion come through whether or not your audience is inspired to engage with your business. It's important to understand and optimize the technical aspects of creating funnels. But it's only one half of the puzzle.

This sparks the argument that the only way for you to get into the market's top 10% you have to connect to your customer. You can't find this from changing the colors of buttons, and re-displaying your ad with a tweak.

Know What Sells

If your opt-ins aren't converting, it means that your audience doesn't want your stuff. That means that you have to make your stuff entirely different than before. When it comes to passive income, it's not all about changing "hidden" out with "secret" in our ads. It's about creating new benefits in ways that get the customer amped up.

SearchEngineLand declared that in order to break into the top 25% of the market, you should do comprehensive research to develop four ads around major areas of interest inside of your market. If you want to convert higher than ten, it's going to take about 10 landing pages to get a good comprehension towards the winning recipe for your income system.

Testing is the backbone of making money online. The more you dive in and learn about what your industry loves and hates, the more ways you're going to find a way to connect with a customer. Research allows you to build a dynamic "empathy" map that allows you to fluently understand your customers.

Have you ever dealt with a support representative from another country? It can lead to confusion and cause frustration for everyone through different dialects and accents.

In a way, if you're not out actively testing your machine up front, you're going to be speaking a foreign accent with your customers. They'll be able to understand you, but your dialect will cause a disconnect in the rapport that you're trying to develop with a new visitor.

By giving yourself the advantage of understanding your industry, you'll be giving yourself a way to fluently connect to potential customers. At the end of the day, it isn't all about fancy marketing strategies. It's all about understanding what the market demands and supplying solutions in a friendly, understanding, and entertaining manner.

The one cool part about passive income is that **people buy from who they like**. If you choose to make a passive income around your hobbies, you'll quickly discover that you can share your entertainment with others from around the world. What's better is that it makes you more money.

Before we move on, it's important to understand the power of having a landing page that converts over 10%. According to SearchEngineLand, the top ten percent of the landing pages in the market actually end up generating about eighty percent of the traffic that rolls through the market. In order to thrive in passive income, all you have to do is find something that somebody wants and give it to them.

Research is Money

If you set out to make a passive income machine around one of your strengths, you'll notice that you can more quickly discover what machines to build and understand where to put them. Researching may feel overwhelming, but it's not. It's actually a pretty simple process once you get the hang of it!

Easy steps to research your market.

1. Find out who's buying ads.
2. Discover how long they've been using the ads. If an ad has been running for a year, it's clearly successful.
3. Build a collection of the passive income

machines that are working.

4. Look around social media and see what people are paying attention to.
5. Plug in a solution and make your own ad around the important areas inside of the industry.
6. Create multiple funnels and ads.
7. Test.
8. Discover what works BEST first. Then fine tune and improve on your winner through even more testing!
9. Move on to the next system.

It's actually as simple as that. Model great businesses and use their powerful knowledge as the foundation for your own ideas and build off of it. In order to win, you can't be a copycat. You can learn from the best though

Developing A Successful Attitude

Now that we understand how important it is to create machines that work well for us, it's time to engage inside of a few rules that you can use to shape your journey on your path to passive glory. In order to succeed in business, you're going to have to treat your passive income machines like a series of workers for your business. With that comes an entirely different world than what we're used to if we aren't entirely self-employed.

Here are some major differences between running a business and being employed.

YOU BEAR ALL RESPONSIBILITY:

When you choose to venture over to passive income, you hold literally all of the responsibility of whether or not you succeed or fail. You can't blame your teachers, your strategies, circumstances, or bad luck. You bear the load of the entire operation's success and failure. Every income machine operates as a result of the quality of work you put into it. Not your teachers, your audience reactions, or the structure of the landing page.

If you firmly believe you don't know what to do after your first trial, pick up this incredible $7 product from Ryan Deiss.

It's called the 21 day launch plan and it's specifically designed to get you your first sale within 21 days of starting the program. This will allow you to get a good feel about how to structure products and services as well as e-commerce stores. It's $7 with a 60 DAY money back guarantee.

However, don't overlook this cheap price tag. If you're uncomfortable on anything related to generating a sale, this will help you every step of the way. It'll show you how to every aspect about building a sales pitch that converts.

These strategies are tested through $15,000,000 in ad testing and a billion emails over the course of three years. In other words, it's a one stop solution that you know will work.

If you feel like you have a good hold on online business, feel free to cruise along the rest of this book and get to work! There's a lot of incredible information you can use to launch passive income machines. But remember, only you are responsible for whether or not you succeed and fail. If you're not 100% positive, you can get an easy to use blueprint for $7.

http://www.digitalmarketer.com/lp/the-21-day-launch-plan/

Work Smart. Not Hard.

Hard work is going to be rewarded as you start launching a series of passive income machines in your spare time. But it isn't going to be what makes or breaks success around business.

While bosses appreciate how hard employees work, customers do not.

They care about one thing, and that's themselves. It's easy to overlook this little aspect when we cruise through building passive income machines.

It's really easy to think all you have to do is buckle up and get to work. Some great people have faced some tough challenges as they started business, and it serves as a clear reminder that the only thing that makes or breaks a business is how many people are converted into positive cash flow.

Two identical people could work different ways for 90 days and have an entirely different outcome. One person can quit his job, but the other feels like he may be stuck at his job forever. What's worse is that the person who's financially independent through passive income only worked 14 hours a week while the gentlemen frustrated about his job worked 30 hours on top of his current work schedule.

But what was the difference?

Well there could be a thousand reasons

actually. But the one major defining factor to achieving financial independence comes through developing an automated system that makes money.

When we dive in, we can look and see that a combination of the right offer to the right audience was more than enough to tip the scale.

However, little factors in attitude actually shift when we don't try to get the most work done. In otherwise identical approaches and skills, the person who quit his job approached every action with a simple thought. "What's the quickest way I can use an asset and convert it into a sale?"

Your Passive Income Machines

Optimizing the money that you make for every second that you will be another major factor in defining how successful you're going to be at generating income. When it comes down making money online, the best way to approach your actions is through this specialized lens.

"What is the fastest way I can launch a high-quality income machine?"
"What is the quickest way I can launch this successful piece of my passive income machine?"

This will allow you to work smart. Because the truth of the matter is why would you spend extra time doing something if your output is relatively the same.

In order to capitalize on this idea and apply it to making passive income, all you have to do is simply focus on getting your business to a specific tier. Are you looking to launch yourself into the top ten percent or are you happy with getting good numbers?

When you're beginning your journey, it's probably best to use these 3 Tiers for your business.

Tier 1: The top 10%.

Tier 2: The top 25%.

Tier 3: Average.

Obviously, there are major jumps in conversion rates. The higher you get in the rankings, the more money you will make with every visitor to your website. However, this doesn't mean that you need to become a perfectionist when it comes to conversion.

Remember that great money can be made from hitting the top half of businesses inside of your industry! There's benefits of every tier in terms of generating great $/hr income.

Tier 3:

If you quickly launch specialized campaigns in an average way, you can combine the data that you get from the industry in order to create a higher tier service and ad. However, the major drawback to the third tier is that this takes time, and you lose out on the initial results you would gain from spending just 25 hours heavily researching your market.

The third tier is also considered as a great way to get your first couple of income streams rolling. It's nice to see results fast, and that's exactly what you get through blasting through your research and immediately developing a functioning advertisement for your service. Placing your focus along the third tier also presents another great advantage for beginners.

With the development of advertising platforms through social media, you can test your passive income streams with very little money before you blast them out. As a result, you'll find that you can create better conversions through the ability to compile more information about your traffic and advertisements in a shorter time frame.

This method also allows you to free up extra income through the use of sales. As a word of caution, never spend money that hasn't been confirmed as a sale. For example, if you have a 30 day risk-free trial period, you have to wait 30 days until you can access the sale.

That doesn't sound all that appetizing, but it can save you from a nightmare. Over time, you'll learn more about the averages of your money, and you can prepare for worst case scenarios with ease. But for now, it's understandable to want to immediately reinvest. However, you have to remember that you have a very small sample for how your numbers are going to turn out over 1,000 customers. It's even more crucial to look towards the perspective that you have absolutely no clue to what the refund rate is like until you've received 1,000 consumers.

Tier 2:

The second tier also offers an insanely unique set of gifts and rewards. If you sit down and think about the time it would take to design an advertisement, you'd be surprised at how quickly you can build one.

All it takes to develop a series of tier two advertisements is the ability to understand what the market wants to buy, and then to bring a unique way to capture some attention towards supplying your demand.

If you're looking to build tier 2 passive income funnels, it's best to dive into something that you enjoy and you have a decent knowledge around. This is due to the challenges that are faced in developing funnels that convert at high rates. In order to get a competitive edge inside of the market, the more information you have in your arsenal the better.

Plus, why wouldn't you launch a passive income machine around a place where you both enjoy working and understand well. It makes your interests more entertaining and allows you to master something you enjoy! This basic foundation is what will lead you into the second tier inside of your projects.

It's also important to note, that you can use a combination of 3 tier passive income systems while 2 tiers are working for you at the same time. This is the beauty of passive income machines. The more work you put in up front, the more money you'll make over time.

The second tier is just as flexible when it comes to the third. You'll find the same perks revolving around your opportunity to diversify small investments before you expand from your successful ideas.

The second tier is also the best tier for discovering first tier products and services. It allows you to test, understand and get feedback around important areas inside of your industry. This will allow you to create another powerful competitive edge as you progress through your newer passive income systems.

Remember that the third tier is wonderful because it's profitable. But the more quickly you dive in to develop products and advertisements that revolve around what your market is already responding to, the faster you're going to make money.

Tier 3:
Third tier solutions are the magic bullets that we discover that solve specific solutions to problems that are extremely important to the customer. For example, a 15 minute routine to permanently cure insomnia would make an absolute killing. Third tier products are the tickets to the kingdom inside of success throughout the life of the important factors of success.

However, third tier solutions don't grow on trees. They require comprehensive approaches to create simple, but cutting-edge solutions. But they can't be any epic solution. It has to be the solution that drives the entire market at the very core.

These home runs take time to develop, but when they are discovered it's time to throw money at it like a tech investor would through his money into raising technologies in major industries (Investing is a wonderful example of passive income!).

There is one extreme disadvantage to having only one third-tier product. In order to successfully capitalize on an advertisement, we have to be able to invest inside of it. It's kind of like the holy grail of passive income.

You simply put money into a robot that works for you around the clock, and you get money.

However, the competition inside of the markets are fierce. Someone will discover your secret and use it against you. This means that you have a small window to launch innovative products inside of your market place.

Your competition pays attention, and they aren't afraid to compete. If you don't have the money to spark a wave of social media buzz around your product and your business, word won't ever actually spread.

Instead, your competition will use the same advantage you had and model your solution. Then they bring it into the spotlight and make a killing from your idea.

In other words, the moment that you discover you have a sure-fire winner is the moment you need to put a good portion of your investing money on deck.

As a beginner, if you discover one of these great ads, it's best to move your advertisement through Facebook in order to keep your ads a little more hidden from your competition. After you test over 1,000 customers, you'll have enough of a sample size to find an investor.

It Shouldn't Feel Like Work

There's a major difference between executing an automated mini business and working for your employer. While being successful is completely up to you, that doesn't mean that you have to be a serious person while you develop your business. Your passive income funnels are supposed to be fun!

Have fun engaging in your system and trying new advertising ideas out. It can be easy to get caught up in professionalism when you first become a professional. It causes us to get technical and creates a major disconnect with your audience.

By having fun while you create your automated machines, you're giving yourself a chance to break out of your shell and learn more about any subject that you're passionate about. Go out there and explores your option! There are thousands of ways to make money online, but the only way to get there is to make something valuable.

What's the most valuable use of our free time? To have fun! That's what consumers love. They love to enjoy their day through the consumption of media. Find a way to get yourself on that map by having fun. If you're too serious, you'll have a major disconnect with your audience and your advertisements will be less impactful.

Always Stay True to the Customer

Always do what's best for the clients that

choose to put faith in your business, and make sure you give them an even better reason to put faith in you before you sell something. Customers honestly aren't greedy.

If they see an experience they enjoy, they generally tend to invest money in it if they have access to it. By staying in tune with your audience, understanding what's important to them and helping them along their way through life, you'll unlock some great secrets to making a big difference in someone's life.

By focusing on giving customers what they are consciously focusing on will allow you to naturally increase the value of your automatic income funnels. Remember that you only end up touching one of your income funnels once before you set it off on autopilot to make money for you. You don't want to have to work your life away to earn a second income. However, it's best to remember that the systems that you build work automatically without any effort on your part.

Aside from checking in once a week, the funnel you built is working great! Now you can focus on a new industry, product, solution, or service while your current passive income machine makes you money!

Reviewing Your Profitable Passive Income Machines

Passive income machines are incredible! But it doesn't mean that they don't need to be maintained. It's important to understand that passive isn't entirely true when it comes to set and forget. When we invest in a business, it goes to work for us to prove that your investment in them was worthy. This happens through a team of brilliant men and women working hard to make sure their business thrives.

When you set up passive incomes, it's important to remember that demands shift throughout every industry. Once we have some nice money in the bank from our income machines, we have to make sure that our ads are performing accurately and doing a little competitive research to see how you're comparing to your competition.

Over a couple of months of studying successful businesses, you'll be able to see how they work. You'll start understanding what competitive edges your business has and what great things your competition does. It's crazy to ignore what fellow experts are saying, so keep up to date and engage a little bit every week.

If you fail to keep up with your incomes, your market could dry up without your knowledge.

Every investment is an important key towards developing financial independence. It's important to give it its fair share. Plus, every hour you spend inside of your industry gives you more knowledge and allows you to make at least one more ad and product to test.

By tapping into what you currently have and analyzing it in depth, you'll be able to create innovations inside of ways to get yourself into the spotlight. And in the modern media, social kills. You don't need millions of dollars to access viewers. Anyone can start a successful business. All it takes is getting started

Don't Let Failure Strike Fear in Your Heart.

Putting valuable time, hard work and our self-confidence on the line definitely leaves room for fear to strike some sense into your heart. What if you fail?

Everybody stumbles. Especially in online business. That doesn't mean that you don't have what it takes to win. A fear of failure can hold you back, and every second that you waste away is a loss in compounding.

You need to be knowledgeable around your passive income streams, but that doesn't mean you have to make slow and methodical solutions that are thoroughly planned. When every successful company comes into a new market, they actually go in expecting to fail to discover what the customer wants.

We can use the valuable information we

know about the market, but until we actually go live, you never know what could happen.

What if you put valuable money on the line, and your ads don't work?

If you're worried about losing money, simply throw in $10 to see if you get a bite. While the sample size may not be big enough to create a verdict, you can get a nice feel for how things are going. The important part of automating your income is taking action as quick as possible so you can get a robot working for you around the clock while you make another one!

What if your first couple machines don't work. Not every idea is a winner, and that's fine. The only way to actually discover what works is to get the feedback required to improve your passive income funnel. In other words, you're investing money up front so you can discover big winners in the future.

If you come in with the perspective that you're going to invest "x" dollars every month, you get the awesome benefit of creating more successful products in the future. When you balance out your first couple monthly losses against the success of the positive ads you ran as a result, you'll discover that your major boost in conversion was well worth having an income machine that worked good enough.

In other words, if you rack up a few losers, you're heading towards a winner from different advertising strategies and core emotional drivers inside of the market.

Fear will kill your dreams at increasing your income while you sleep. Don't let it take over your ability to take action and get things done. At the end of the day, success in passive income comes from getting things up and running. That's a far cry from worrying about whether or not we can do it in the first place. Don't let your beliefs and fears trap you inside of a box. Your emotions don't even want you to fail in the first place. Make sure you implement high quality stuff inside of your business, but also make timely decisions and do exactly what you need to in order to automate the action you're taking.

The faster you throw something of high

quality out for feedback, the faster it makes you money.

Be Confident, But Keep Your Ego in Check!

You have to believe that you can successfully make money for you to actually make the money in the first place. But that doesn't mean you have to be even slightly pretentious about the gravity of the situation. When an audience engages with your business, it's a fantasy compared to the world where you pull weight to become a delightful addition to your company and bosses.

However, unlike your bosses, someone who's looking to improve their life or have fun don't feel like getting bragged to. Not even in the slightest bit. If you're launching a product on how do something epic, actually have fun doing it instead of focusing on the importance of the situation. You don't actually connect with your audience. The audience connects itself with you.

Remember you'll only make money passively if people are digging what you're selling. So if a portion of your audience can't connect with you because they don't trust you, you'll be better off moving your time and assets elsewhere. You can't give people something they want by building a series of negative associations around you. If someone travels to your site, and doesn't like you, they're probably going to buy that same exact thing elsewhere.

So be kind, connect, and have fun. Don't

develop the lecturer's mentality.

Take the Time and Energy to Create Feedback from Your Audience.

Not everyone new to passive income has been taught a practice on the retention of customers. Someone giving attention to you is the perfect time to find a way to collect feedback. Get to know your customers and see what they thought about your pitches and ideas.

Sometimes the biggest marketing breakthroughs happen inside of one-on-one conversations. You never really know what people choose not to disclose in public, and you can actually build a powerful bridge of trust if you take the time to see how you can improve their experience and their lives.

The Only Time to Work Harder Is After You Lose.

A common approach to passive income is to overwork and to throw everything in on the very first shot. This can cause a lot of unwanted feelings of failure and can blast a major shot to our self-confidence.

During moments like these, the only thing to do is to work harder. Jump right in and see why it didn't work, and then make something new immediately from what you've discovered. Remember, it takes feedback from about 10 well thought out ad tests to produce a winner. Why would you just quit after one or two?

There are a lot of times in life when we feel like giving up. Being your own boss is the easy life. But not every moment is heaven on Earth. When you get hit with a loss, use it as motivation to work harder. It means that you're that much closer to a winning ad! If you use the emotional drivers of any market, you'll find a nice winner eventually!

When it doesn't work, simply pound away and fix it. As a business owner, it's important to develop a mindset where the moment you discover something isn't working, you take direct action to get it to work.

Where would your attitude be then? Probably not so optimistic. Putting in 50 hours of work to lose money isn't pleasant. But the bitter truth is simple. It's much more important to get out there and fail, because you'll have direct feedback about what you need to do to fix the problem.

If you simply try to over plan and perfect your passive income funnels, you may spend months only to run into the same exact invisible problem you encountered with your first version of your plan.

The only way to get the information you need to become successful is to create **feedback**.

The only way to get feedback is to take action and possibly fail.
The passive income game isn't about whether or not you'll fail. It's about what you do when you do fail. Are you going to

give up or are you going to fight through more ads or products to find a winning recipe?

Successful Product Ideas

Everyone encourages making some great products to sell off. Let's face it. You make a killing off of virtual products and services. It's nuts.

However, having a product doesn't do any good if you don't know what you're doing. In fact, it makes matters worse. Why?

Let's look towards a common misconception about making a product. Let's say you make a ground-breaking course and you want to sell it for $100. You throw up the advertisement and it flops.

But why?
Well there's 3 options and one is more terrible than the other.

1. You don't have a good marketing strategy and you don't connect with the customer.
2. Your product sucks in your customer's eyes.
3. Your product and ad is awesome, but you don't price your product properly.

Imagine what would happen if you experienced the third problem on your first go. Imagine if you whiffed on your first launch and you began testing new ads. Those didn't work so you changed the product and went back to the old ads. It didn't work. As a result, you try another ad trying to figure out why it didn't sell.

This is a nightmare of a situation. You worked hard, did everything right, and you lost three investments in a successful campaign after you did everything great!

This leads us to think pretty simplistically about creating a new product or service around the successful foundations of your competition.

It's actually pretty nice to be able to make money from your competitors when you first start out. It will allow you to get a grip on the deeper drivers inside of your market. Plus, you'll get a lot of free marketing information from a superstar performing product. What's there not to like?

After you make money from someone else's products, you can make money from your own. But if you're just beginning, why not make the quickest amount of money with the time that you're putting into work. Plus, by the time you're successfully making money, you may not even want to create a product until you have a bigger list!

Be Responsible with Your Budget

Studies show that even wealthy people can become financially stressed. People just have a natural inclination to spend what money they have.

In order for you to actually make an impact in your life through creating passive income, it's probably best to take control of your spending while you're in the process of making income systems to run money. Let's face it. The reality is harsh around money. We have to take control of our spending and consciously inspect where we're spending our money and our time.

If you're under financial stress currently, it's due to the fact of how you choose to invest your resources. If you simply make more money without fixing your spending leaks, the places you lose money now will only inflate in the future. Everyone loves to have nice things and to enjoy life. But it's also important to make sure that you have a nice grip inside of your finances.

The more you can do with your resources now creates a situation where you can speed up your compounding in the future. The only way for you to make good money off of income streams is to expand and create more money through reinvesting your returns immediately. The more seriously you treat your budget, the more you'll be rewarded from your positive investment machines.

Every dollar you invest adds up big over time.

Compounding is the primary tool of every professional passive income expert.
If you keep dipping into your profits, it's time to inspect and make a plan to make sure you have extra money to invest rather than dipping into the money you need to reinvest. This can come in various forms and every situation is unique.

However, it's important to clarify that in order to succeed in the business, you have to be financially responsible. The only way to increase your current income is to invest your current income to receive the highest returns we can as quickly as possible.

Remember that we don't have a blog that can let us go viral. Our marketing comes primarily from investment in order for us to save more time in the future.

As a passive income creator, your goal isn't to be savvy or smart. It's to make money as easily and as quickly as possible.
One great ad for one great product is more than enough to get you started. But in order for you to progress you need to invest as much money into the system as fast as possible. Through living your current situations out at a profit, every month you'll be able to increase your monthly income through raising the amount of money we throw into our income funnel.

Get Things Done!

The only way to be successful in this business is to get things done. In order for you to get moving you have to have a plan to get you exactly where you want to go, and you have to execute in order to produce results.

If you simply approach passive income when you have the time, you're probably going to let other things interfere with your desire to make some extra income. Through setting an exact set of times inside of your week that you're going to dedicate to creating a passive income stream, you'll actually have the plan laid out in stone in front of you.

Something magical happens when you see

your goals set in stone. If you're serious about making money, the only way to set a schedule is through choosing how many hours you need to work and to build a practical schedule for you to work on your profits.

Ideally, you'd like to dedicate time every day if possible. The quicker your present moment is filled with actions towards generating a passive income, the quicker you're going to actually acquire the passive income. Your life is a series of present moments. Address your passive income goals as soon as you can. Every time you get an opportunity to take action, do it now! There's no better time than the present than to accomplish your goals towards automating machines!

Through allotting time throughout your life, you'll be able to quickly and efficiently build automated income. But the truth is that you have to get to work as often as you can in order to fulfill your goals of becoming financially independent.

Set a SMART Goal

SMART goal setting is an incredible way for you to use your time as you work your way through building income funnels. By giving yourself a specific date for your deadline, you'll be able to work towards your monetary goals while you focus on the task at hand.

If you're not sure exactly how you're going to do things, time will slip away from you. Having a static amount of money you'd like to make within your first 90 days is a great way to start. While beliefs are a powerful force, it's important to set realistic expectations inside of your workflow.

Set a nice and practical goal for your progress over the first 90 days of work. Maybe you'd like 3 fully automated systems bringing in $1,000 a month. Maybe you have money to invest and you're looking for $10,000. No matter how practical you think your goal is, the best way to set a realistic goal is through looking at how much money (or time) you have to invest every month.

This will give you a realistic guideline of the type of money you're going to be making. If you don't have any money to invest, you have time. A great place to use as a reference would be your current income level, or the income level that you're most accustomed to.

While you can easily make more than this through practical applications of automation, there's no doubt that you'd be happy with doubling your income over the course of a year's time. Now is the perfect time to start so you can get to where you want to be in 90 days.

Your upcoming work is going to be a series of present moments, so make sure you have systems to stop you from skipping business sessions. If you want to do business first thing in the day, simply wake up, eat breakfast and train yourself to sit directly in your seat. Sometimes the hardest part about getting things done is simply doing it when you have the moment. Don't use your ability to plan to do things later to help you start your mission towards passive income. This will lead to inconsistent sessions, and scattered accomplishments.

Through taking advantage of the moments that you have in life to work on your dreams, you'll be able to take a wonderful approach towards success.

Whatever your brain is tuned to is the perfect goal to set. It will allow your subconscious mind to work with what you've given it in order to create a situation that's familiar.

Tailor Your System for You

Along the way, you're going to find something that you're not great at, or you're going to discover that you absolutely hate doing something. The goal of a good passive income system is to have fun.

By understanding what you enjoy doing, you'll be able to keep your momentum rolling. And if you identify something that you're not good at, you can hire someone that can do it for you.

Never get stuck in the way that things should be. Look at the things that you love to do and how you can translate that into fulfilling your financial goal. This will lead you down paths that you didn't think about previously. By keeping your eye on the prize, you'll side step nightmares so you can work towards your goal.

If you get wrapped up in hating doing one thing, you're probably not going to come back to work as often. Let's face it. We do things that we enjoy. By having fun, you're getting yourself one step closer towards acquiring some great passive income. A business that revolves around the enjoyment of the industry you're working on is a business that customers love.

Build a Portfolio

No matter what passive income funnel you choose to use, using it to build an overall portfolio for your company will transform the amount of opportunities that you have down the line. By clearly understanding exactly what you have accomplished and what you know how to do, you'll open up a new world of possibilities for your business. Maybe you'd like a loan. Maybe you want to interview experts around the field. Maybe you want to launch a bestselling course.

Everything that you make has a value and even if it doesn't make money, it can serve the foundations for better opportunities down the road. If you approach everything you launch as an asset you can sell off in the future, you'll be ahead of the competition.

Portfolios allow us to communicate with businesses that have major audiences, and they also allow us to build our own value and image for our brands. Using this attitude will force you to consistently produce the best work you can as you progress through your passive income machines.

If you work hard, keep up, and have fun,

you'll find that you have a vast network of "businesses" working for you around the clock.

Start Networking with Other Passive Income Machine Owners

After you start to get the ball rolling and you have a few income funnels rocking, you can choose to get out there and get some free exposure for your income funnels.

There are tons of great ways you can help others while you earn money from your funnels. You can start building Facebook pages, Instagram accounts, and other social media channels. The truth is that once you have a system that makes money, the more people that come through your website are going to directly relate to the amount of sales you're going to generate.

Realize that every way you can find an

audience is unique and has a different preference towards the way thing are presented. For example, some traffic sources tend to procrastinate while other traffic sources have incredibly busy lives.

There's a whole industry out there waiting for you! While you're waiting on your investments to deliver results, you can start gaining traction through answering questions with others and hosting live events on Facebook and YouTube. Find out what you love to do and what your market enjoys most and match your skills to provide the audience with things that they crave. Are videos big? Do you hate being in front of the camera? Hire someone to read the script for you on Fiverr.

Once your income machines start to make money, you can meet up and hangout with top experts around the field and even exchange guest posts to websites. In business, all exposure is good when you stay focused on making a good product and helping your industry improve lives.

Attend Major Community Events

Going to major events inside of your industry is another wonderful way for you to make a splash. With live news and coverage, you can keep your fans up to date with what's happening at the events, and the exciting things that you have in store.

Major events are filled with networking opportunities for some of your favorite brands! By attending these events as a business, you get to hang out and possibly earn a way to make some more money by landing a featured interview!

Putting yourself in the spotlight gives you some great authority and can make or break your events worth hundreds of times the value of the trip. This probably won't happen often, but getting yourself out there and active will give you credibility to your current clients and will attract new streams of money inside of the future.

Remember that every action you take can be used inside of your portfolio as you build your passive income streams. Every time you're out there having a blast with some of your favorite idols, your passive income systems will be working hard for you. That's a pretty cool place to be in. Every time you land on someone's website, channel or blog, you stay there forever. That's the power of networking. Imagine having your business featured even in one of the top 25 businesses inside of the industry!

You Don't Have to Say Yes to Anything

Another power that comes with being your own boss is that you're in control of when you say no. Our careers can put us in some uncomfortable situations. Maybe you met a fan and you over commit your time for the weekend. Maybe you're juggling a dozen projects at once.

The truth is that you can't really do something until the thing you have to currently address is done.

By saying yes too much, you'll actually decrease the amount of the great passive machines you put out, and you'll decrease the quality of every single machine that you make. It's important to work hard in life, but you have to understand that your brain really does have limitations.

Your natural body cycles actually like it if you take a 20 minute break after every 90 minutes of work. If you take a week off, you feel more refreshed coming back into your groove.

In order to be successful, you don't have to max out your schedule. It's nice to have opportunities, but there honestly is more out there than you can handle. Learn when you're at max capacity and book up your business ventures for later down the road.

The fact that you're doing so much for your business will actually make people even more excited to schedule a great time to work.

Discover A Major Passive Asset Like Full Websites

After you're making some money with easy opportunities, you'll start getting excited about the magnitude of having a flagship product. Throughout your endeavors, you've probably discovered a killer idea and it's loved by your consumers. There are the perfect opportunities for us to re-brand, reformat, and repackage our content into a major launch.

If you choose to launch a website, you can use all of the networking and connections in order to launch a huge product. This will help you make splashes inside of your industry. The best part is that if you paid attention to building your portfolio, you're going to end up with a bunch of hype for your website. You'll get lots of visitors, lots of sales, and life will be wonderful.

There are a lot of incredible opportunities out there to make money through passive income. If you work hard and treat your funnels like a professional, you're going to get noticed. This will give you a chance to become an authority and a trusted adviser. Jay Abraham says that your world changes when your customers transform from money into people that love being around your business.

Being well liked from your passive income funnels will give you even more assets as you collect a sustainable customer base. You can begin showcasing other businesses as an affiliate, and other businesses can direct their customers over to your flagship product.

Life is good when you have a great portfolio with an awesome reputation.

Beyond Your First Successful Passive Income Source

Life is too short to contemplate. If you're looking to become successful at creating a passive income, only you can discover what the right path is. Before you dive in, spend a couple of hours to really discover what you enjoy. Ask yourself if you could do anything for your job, what would you do? Take that answer and find a way to launch a passive income funnel around.

When you dive into taking action, it can be a little bit scary at first. Luckily, there is a ton of free resources available. Maybe you love drawing and you discover you want to make money through drawing!

You discover that there's this amazing drawing course and you choose to enroll and start a collection of articles around the things that you learned throughout your journey. You can then use these major assets to promote the online course and make great money by working with your competitors.

The cool thing is that you can choose to do a lot with the information that you learned while you played. Maybe you'd like to advance further and teach others how to draw by making your own drawing video course. Maybe you just want to make a coloring book.

No matter where your journey takes you, someone has been down your path and has left a clue on how to do things. All it takes to succeed is a little bit of passion, an understanding of getting things done, and a system that generates money.

If you're ever unsure of exactly where to go if you need to research, there are thousands of resources around online if you look close enough. Academics and scholars from all over the world have shared information that can "only" be acquired through master's degrees.

All you have to do is search and discover who is the cutting-edge person in the field. Google is a wonderful source to find reputable businesses inside of big markets. You can also look at companies that sell on Amazon. If you need an expert, you can look towards professors in open classrooms at MIT. You can learn how to develop an app from Google through Udemy.

All it takes to learn something is to find the best person in the business that has a specialty in what you're trying to do. If there isn't anyone that can do what you're trying to, use trial and error and become that specialist!

There are thousands of chances out there to make money while you play on vacation and during the times that you need to rest. Whatever your motivation and your goal, this book was designed to get you taking action. There's no doubt that you want to make money through launching passive income machines.

The best way to get there is to take action as

quickly as possible to get things done. Do you know what business you're going to run? Do you know what industry you're looking at? Are you clueless around a subject or are you fluent in it? What do you know about the market? What don't you know about it? What natural gifts do you have? How can you use these natural gifts to take advantage of making passive income?

Is there a hobby you'd love to learn? There's a thousand ways to approach business. The important part is to know exactly what you need to do. This book has given you the foundation of tools that are needed in order to succeed once you discover which road that you need to take to install your first passive income machine.

Remember that if you don't know where to go from here, you can try out The 21 Day Action Plan from DigitalMarketer and try to make your first sale 21 days from now!

www.ingramcontent.com/pod-product-compliance
Lightning Source LLC
Chambersburg PA
CBHW070103210526
45170CB00012B/724